Online Advertising Made Simple for Trucking

Landon Middleton

Online Advertising Made Simple for Trucking
Copyright © 2017 by Landon Middleton.

All rights reserved. No part of this book may be reproduced or transmitted in any form or by any means without written permission of the author.

Limit of Liability/Disclaimer of Warranty: While the publisher and author have used their best efforts in preparing this book, they make no representations or warranties with respect to the accuracy or completeness of the contents of this book and specifically disclaim any implied warranties of merchantability or fitness for a particular purpose. No warranty may be created or extended by sales representatives or written sales materials. The advice and strategies contained herein may not be suitable for your situation. You should consult with a professional where appropriate. Neither the publisher nor the authors shall be liable for any loss of profit or any other commercial damages, including but not limited to special, incidental, consequential, or other damages.

Table of Contents

Foreword	4
1. Why on Earth Would You Read This?	9
2. The PPC Lead Driving System For Trucking	13
3. Pop the Hood: What Are You Selling?	18
4. Lock Down Your Landing Pages	25
5. Hit the Highway with PPC	44
6. On the Horn with PPC	57
7. Your Ads Require Regular Tune-Ups	70
8. How To Work With Us	77
About the Author	86

FOREWORD

In the small business world, many individuals are AMAZING at what they do or sell. However, when it comes down to marketing their products or services, it's an additional skillset few business owners have. But what if you could be one of them? Before you roll your eyes in disbelief, you owe it to yourself to read *Online Advertising Made Simple for Trucking*. Seriously, set aside some time and let Landon walk you through what over a decade of experience has taught him regarding how to maximize your marketing efforts inside the trucking industry.

Also, ask yourself this: If someone questioned you about your marketing ROI, PPC strategies, and preferred platforms, would you even know where to start?

If so, great! But even then, can you honestly say there is no room for improvement? And when was the last time someone with over ten years of industry experience offered to teach you the top tricks of their trade? What have you got to lose? Nothing.

And, if you're like the majority of trucking companies out there, you might not recognize more than one (or maybe two) of the items I mentioned above. I want to pause here, and emphasize just how normal that is. It's nothing to be ashamed of, and something 95% of small business owners struggle with. No one can be great in every aspect of a business. It's just not humanly possible.

After all, you've specialized in what you need to know to match cargo to trucks, and drivers to destinations. You've probably spent years building your business and growing your expertise, right? Well, Landon has spent those same years focused on how to deliver a step-by-step marketing results strategy for trucking companies just like yours. And it works.

The book you're holding is an industry insider's guide to maximizing your company's Pay Per Click (PPC) marketing program. Built on numerous years of experience in both the information technology (IT) industry and the trucking industry, Landon walks you through all the key components of a successful PPC strategy, and everything you need to consider in order to implement them correctly.

Plus, it's all written down for you in plain English – not IT jargon.

But, how are we defining success? Through results. I mean actual, measurable improvements in both your revenue and return on investment – because in the end, that's all that really counts.

Think about it this way... If you aren't getting the marketing bang for your buck that you expected (or you wish you could stretch those limited marketing dollars just a little bit farther), this is the action plan you need to accomplish those goals. If you want more customers, more drivers, and more of the results you want to see, (and the extra cash that comes with them) then keep on reading.

Now, perhaps you've heard that "pay-per-click" is a bad word in the marketing world. And in some instances, you'd be 100% right. It's not easy or simple. Most companies struggle to do it right, and it becomes an expensive experiment for them. However, the right PPC campaign, paired with the right tools, can deliver significant results for a fraction of the cost.

Here are ten ways this book will help you get rolling:
1. It provides industry expertise, written in an actionable and easy to understand way.
2. It hones in on the essence of what you're actually selling (spoiler alert: it's NOT trucking!).

Foreword

3. Illustrates the difference between a company and a customer focus.
4. Provides the Internet building blocks you need for success, and how landing pages fit into the picture.
5. Outlines the online habits and tendencies of everyday customers.
6. Helps you create keywords to drive action.
7. Demonstrates what a good landing page needs to convert browsers into leads.
8. Overviews proper ad campaign structure.
9. Provides a plan to close, ensuring those leads turn into real customers.
10. Helps you understand how to refine and revise your strategy as time goes on.

It really is that simple. And honestly, that hard. But when you have the know-how required to make each of those items a full piece of your marketing strategy, you can't lose.

Your trucking business needs every advantage it can get, right? Use this guide to educate yourself about the intricacies of PPC marketing, and how it might benefit you. Read it. Re-read it. Digest it. Understand it. Then take what you've learned and think about how you can apply it to your own business. This thorough and comprehensive guide could be worth thousands of dollars to your business – but only if you take action.

And the best part? Landon's decades of experience are available to you, every step along the way. Whether you leverage his knowledge inside the guide or opt to have him build your custom campaign from start to finish, his expertise is exactly what you need to take your business to the next level.

Now, the only question that remains is: Are you ready to get started?

Terry Lewis
Director of Sales, Track Point Systems

CHAPTER 1

WHY ON EARTH WOULD YOU READ THIS?

I think we may be a lot alike. We usually only get called when someone realizes something's gone completely haywire, and we come in and fix what's broken. Oh, and, we both serve the noble, hardworking folks that keep the wheels of American commerce rolling.

You fix trucking industry challenges. I fix broken marketing for trucking companies.

You're busy and probably don't want to spend a whole lot of time and energy wading through some massive, technical book and I don't want to write a book that people would rather shred and use to line a litter box than read.

So, how about we make a deal?

I'll lay out for you a practical, actionable plan you can use to get real, no-nonsense results for your trucking business (that means filling trucks, moving freight, and making trucking companies more profitable) in a way that won't leave you preferring to shut a cab door on your thumb – and you give it a quick read. Sound fair?

I should probably introduce myself first. My name is Landon Middleton.

After years working in information technology outside of Oklahoma City, I felt the call to go into full-time ministry, and decided it was time to start a company. I asked around to see what problems people had that I could solve. Search engine optimization looked like a good fit, and to be honest, getting a company onto the first page in Google looked like magic.

Once I got started, my first client recommended me to my second client, who was in the DOT drug testing business. He took me under his wing and taught me all about the trucking industry.

"Once you go trucking, you never go back," David Saunders told me. And he was right. There's this small town feel in our industry... if you do people right, you're in business. Do them wrong, and you better leave town. We attended multiple state association events, got out there advocating on behalf of the carriers and companies in the industry, shook hands, listened to trucking company owners, and I learned the trucking industry inside and out.

While so many trucking companies are dumping money into old school marketing tactics and then praying they'll work, they're working harder and harder to get just a tiny fraction of the results they used to get. And the "R" word? Results are really the only thing that matters, period. That's why trucking and Pay Per Click advertising go so well together.

Trucking and PPC advertising go together like tractors and trailers. Carriers need the phone to ring – a lot – with drivers who are qualified and highly-motivated to drive. Trucking vendors need to be able to get in front of fleets of all different sizes with problems they can solve. And neither of them want to have to pay for leads they don't own, pound the phones, and rely on tired, old tactics that depend on racks at truck stops to grab their prospects' attention.

The crazy thing is, PPC is about the LAST thing most marketing consultants will advise for your trucking company to do. Not because it doesn't work (my clients will tell you it works like magic). Not because it's expensive (wouldn't you trade a dime for a dollar all day long?). Not because it's rocket science (you could do it on your own if you're willing to go through the learning curve, although if you had a risk-free way to try having a pro do it for you, you'd take it).

It's because...
- Very few of them know how to do it.
- They know if they do it wrong, the results will be a crash and burn disaster that's nightmare-worthy.
- They suspect (correctly) there are a LOT of details to successfully managing your PPC.

So not only is PPC the best marketing solution for trucking companies, but by the end of this short book, you'll have the exact "step-by-step" blueprint for how to make the whole thing happen.

CHAPTER 2

THE PPC LEAD DRIVING SYSTEM FOR TRUCKING

"What do we want? More drivers! More trucking customers!

When do we want them? Right now!"

Calls, conversions, customers – more of all of these is good, because they lead to revenue.

Articles, blog posts, click-throughs, and website traffic – these are irrelevant because while they might sound smart, they don't put drivers in your trucks or cash in your pocket.

You don't grow a business by spending money on marketing. You grow by investing in income-producing assets and tools.

If you want better results for your trucking company, and not just a bunch of numbers that look like you've been busy, you will find that Facebook and Google's AdWords advertising platforms are an extremely valuable part of the equation for generating more business. The DBSadvantage PPC Lead Driving System is built on Pay Per Click because it works.

What do I mean by, "It works?"

- It means you finally have driver recruitment down to a reliable science.
- It means you have enough cash flow to run and even expand your business.
- It means you have a proven, automated, lead generation machine that you own and rely on to get new customers every day.

So, what is this strategy?

As an example, do a Google search for a trucking company near you. On the top and right-hand side of your Google results, you might see ads. These are Pay Per Click ads that are run through Google's advertising program, which is called AdWords.

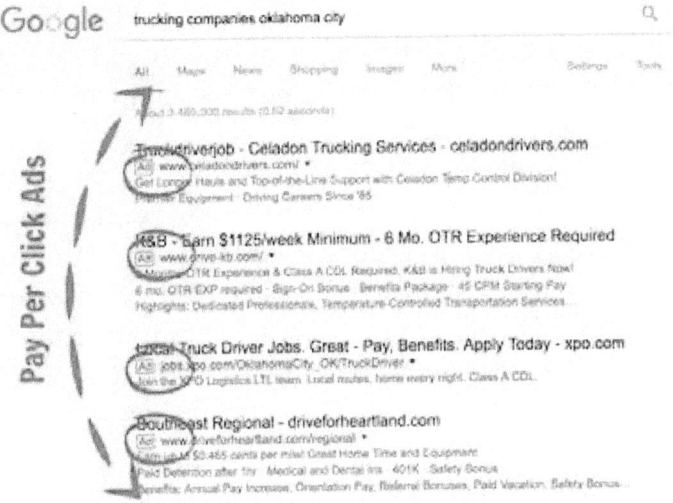

Basically, advertisers bid on keywords they think prospective customers would use to find their products and services. The more targeted the keyword, and the more commercially intended it is (meaning, it's a keyword someone would use when they're looking to buy rather than researching just for kicks), the more likely it is to result in turning a searcher into a real lead.

The advertiser agrees to pay a certain amount every time someone clicks their ad, which is tied to the keywords they're bidding on. Google and Facebook bill advertisers monthly based on how many clicks their ads get.

The ads, when clicked, typically lead searchers to a landing page, which then offers a specific product, service, or opportunity. We'll talk more about landing pages in a bit, but in the case of trucking services, they'll get a name, email and phone number to call for more info, a bit about the company, and maybe even an incentive to call right away.

When using paid advertising, be sure you have a dedicated phone number for your ads and landing pages that's not already associated with your business. This is important for tracking purposes, so you can see exactly how many calls, and what kinds of results these specific ads produce.

Of course, getting calls isn't the end of the story. You'll also need an effective script when answering the phone so you can turn those callers into customers.

The great thing about Pay Per Click and the DBSadvantage PPC Lead Driving System, is that it's so transparent. You set your budget, track your leads and calls, and measure your ROI.

We'll go into more detail about what's needed to build a system like this for your business in the next few chapters, including:
- The 5-step proven process we've used to help double and even triple other trucking companies' revenues.

- How to understand your target market and know for sure what they want.
- How to make sure you've got excellent "message to market match."
- How to know where your prospects are in the buying cycle.
- The difference between buyers versus shoppers versus researchers. This is where Facebook is AMAZING.
- Why it's crucial to "sell the hole rather than the drill."
- How to communicate the benefits your prospects get by doing business with you rather than your competitors.
- The difference between features and benefits.
- How to be customer-focused in your advertising rather than making the same major mistake 99% of trucking companies make.
- How to build high-converting landing pages that Facebook and Google love.
- What keywords and targets work well for the trucking industry – and which are a waste of money.
- What works GREAT when the calls and leads start coming in… and what doesn't.
- How to make tiny changes in your marketing to get HUGE improvements in your results.

Ready?

CHAPTER 3

POP THE HOOD: WHAT ARE YOU SELLING?

You might be under the crazy assumption that your prospects want to apply for a driving job, or worse yet, that you're in the business of selling widgets and services to trucking companies.

Now you're probably thinking, "Well, yeah, dummy!"

But before you jump to conclusions, let me explain.

See, the truth is, your REAL business is solving problems and making life easier.

You are the magic wand that makes frustration disappear. You are the glue that keeps trucking families fed and housed – as well as keeping shelves stocked, supply chains flowing, and people working. Your offerings make entire trucking companies more profitable and secure. You are the knight in shining armor coming to the rescue of townsfolk who are besieged by all sorts of big, bad ogres.

OK, that might be a little much.

But seriously, think about what it means when you hire an excellent driver or make a carrier's business more profitable.

Let's take driver recruitment for example. If great drivers struggle to find quality carriers who are hiring to work for, they end up working for carriers that offer less than wonderful work situations, and after enough frustration, they leave the profession entirely. Without enough excellent drivers on the roads, consumers and businesses enter into a scarcity mode where they're never sure they can get what they need when they need it. Or worse… if the recruitment pickings get slim, carriers end up with less than ideal solutions for filling their cabs – a dangerous situation.

A simple job opening that can't be filled properly adds a ridiculous amount of stress to any carrier's usual load, but also to the other employees and ultimately to the people and communities that depend on timely deliveries.

People don't want to think about the supply chain at all – they just want it to work as expected. They count on it working, not breaking down because you can't find drivers you can count on – or keep your trucks on the road. They're counting on you!

That's what you sell. Reliability.

With that in mind, how well does your advertising match up with what you sell? Does everyone in your business understand your target market of drivers and what they want? Or, trucking companies looking for ways to run more efficiently and cost-effectively? Do you keep this in mind as you sell? Is it at the heart of your marketing?

There's a concept called message to market match. It's about understanding what people want to buy from you, then creating advertising that communicates that that's exactly what you're selling. That message needs to come through loud and clear, with no confusion on your customer's end.

Your market is at the bottom of the funnel.

In marketing, we talk about sales funnels a lot. If you picture a funnel, the guy who doesn't even know he wants what someone's selling is at the top of the funnel. The goal there is to grab his attention and prompt him to start thinking about your product, service, or job opportunity. Once he's interested, we call him a prospect. Aiming your marketing toward prospects isn't the best idea because it can take a long time before they're ready to buy – and the likelihood they'll take action isn't very high.

A bit further down the funnel, you'll find prospects who are doing some research and comparing options. If they were shopping for a new car, this is where they'd be weighing the pros and cons to decide which manufacturer. Also, not the best place to aim your marketing efforts, because it can take them a while to pull the trigger – and a lot can happen between now and then.

At the bottom of the funnel is your sweet spot – the low-hanging fruit, where a prospect is ready to pull the trigger. In a recruitment scenario, these are the people who are actively looking for an opportunity. In the sales cycle, they're at the very last stop before money changes hands. These are the buyers.

Sell the hole, not the drill.

You've probably heard this one before – about the hardware store employee who couldn't sell a drill to save his life. Turns out, the customers didn't care about how many volts the battery was, or how much it weighed, or what kind of torque the drill had.

They didn't just wake up one morning and say, "I think I'll buy a drill today." No, there was a problem that incited this purchase. They didn't need a drill, but a hole.

In the same way, you need to connect with your prospect's real need. Trucking companies don't care about the ten steps you follow to find the best prices on fuel, parts, or repairs. They don't care what certifications and industry memberships you've got. They don't even care about how long you've been in business or how many carriers call on you to solve problems for them. They just want what they want – an excellent driving job, a sweeter bottom line. Now. and a fair price sweetens the deal.

A strange set of balances to strike

Features vs. Benefits

Marketers talk a lot about features and benefits, and which one matters most to customers. Here's a quick explanation:'

Features are the facts about your business, products, and services. For example, you've been in business 25 years. You provide legal assistance to carriers, or fuel discounts, or recourse factoring... or whatever your offer is.

Benefits are what's in it for the customer, why those features matter. For example, let's say you arrange for deep discounts on parts for member fleets. By buying through your program, a carrier enjoys significant savings on name-brand parts, improving their bottom line in a big way.

Company vs. Customer Focus

If you read through most websites – in trucking and other fields as well – you'll probably be shocked to realize how self-centered they are. "We, we, we" they say. We've been in business for X years. We have X number of carriers as customers. We have this certification and won that award. We are the best! Blah, blah, blah.

Your customers don't care about any of that. They just want what they really want! I know, I sound like a broken record – but this is one of the most important keys to getting better results from your marketing. Success means selling people what they want – and what your customers want is a no-hassle experience that ultimately helps them take care of business – and their families.

The details of your business are important, of course. But you want to be sure that in every marketing communication, you keep what matters to your customers as the top priority.

All they really want to know is that they'll get what they need, quickly. Is your price reasonable? Can you get things rolling today? Communicate the right answers to these questions, and you'll find your phones ringing automatically.

Keeping that in mind makes your marketing message a whole lot simpler, doesn't it?

Next, we're going to look at what makes landing pages turn your prospects into eager leads who are ready to do business with you.

CHAPTER 4

LOCK DOWN YOUR LANDING PAGES

Now that we're clear about what you're actually selling, it's time to build a piece of your marketing funnel that communicates that message.

The first pieces to focus on are your landing pages. Yeah, plural. Pages.

You might already be sweating a little, remembering how much fun it was building your website. Or you could be feeling kind of smug, saying, "Ha! I've already got a website! I can skip right over this chapter!"

Sorry.

Your Home page is the hub of your website. Every website is expected to have a Home page. It's the primary page SEO guys aim to optimize. They feature your main keywords there, some text that communicates your visitors are in the right place, and usually a subscription box where they can sign up for your newsletter. The Home page is all about content marketing.

So, it's not what we're talking about right now.

Right now, we're talking about landing pages, where searchers first land on your site.

That clears things up, doesn't it? Just to make it a hair more confusing, many, many businesses out there use their Home page as a landing page. They send all of their traffic to the Home page. From the Home page, they hope their content marketing efforts will work and send visitors deeper into the website to read articles, watch videos and learn about the services they have to offer.

Not at all what we want to do.

Instead, with a landing page, we want to nudge prospects to take action – call or opt-in to get started. Everything on your landing page should assure visitors that they're in good hands, then make it easy for them to call you and more, without ever leaving that page.

Your landing page is a crucial piece of your online sales funnel. We want your prospects flowing through that funnel like it's been greased. No bumps, no bottlenecks, no holes. They slide in and through and come out the other side as your new and very happy customers or drivers. A smooth funnel requires a high-converting landing page.

So, what makes a landing page convert visitors into customers?

There are a few elements your landing pages must have to turn the traffic you get from your PPC ads into hot leads you can close – or hire – easily.

Your Keywords

Remember, your keywords are the words and phrases your leads enter into Google or talk about on Facebook when they go looking for trucking services. You want to focus on ONE keyword for each landing page. Conversely, that also means you'll want a landing page for each keyword or conversation.

What sort of keywords do you use? Well, that depends entirely on your focus as a business. Let's say your company sells aftermarket parts for trucks…

- All the carriers you serve

- All the makes you make parts for

- All the locations you service

- All the combinations of all of the above

One great thing about using landing pages instead of just your Home page is that you can go after long-tail keywords. These are highly specific, multiple-word search terms people look for when they are really, really serious about finding you. Long-tail keywords or conversations might look like this:

Kenworth Truck Accessories Oklahoma City OK

Long, huh? Think whoever types that into Google or talks on Facebook is serious about finding those truck parts? It's not a casual Google search; this person means business. By having a specific page for this search term, one just about Kenworth truck accessories in Oklahoma City, you boost your odds of turning that searcher into your newest customer because they have 100% confidence you can fix their specific problem.

If you were using SEO for marketing, you'd be sunk right about here. Remember, SEO typically aims to compete on a generic keyword level because of the practical limits that come with trying to do content marketing. It's impossible to have enough content ranking high for thousands of keywords – and, again, even if you DID succeed in ranking it high, content is NOT what works best for trucking industry marketing.

By using Google AdWords or Facebook ads, there's complete control over keywords and geo-targeting, which ensures your ads show up only where they'll get results. Also, the ad goes straight to the landing page specific to their problem (instead of your home page which is what happens with SEO.) This level of control enables you to run highly relevant, precisely local ads, with super targeted offers.

The Structure of Your Landing Page

The structure is really important, and can make or break your results. The elements of a high-converting landing page all need to be there, written the right way, formatted the right way, and in the right order. No pressure, right?

Here are those elements:

- **Headline:** It needs to be engaging, reassuring, and action-prompting so your visitors know they're in the right place, you'll take good care of them, and they won't get ripped off.

- **Bullet Points:** Each "bullet" provides more detail – benefit-rich detail. It's a good idea to start each bullet with wording like, "You get…" followed by a benefit they'll enjoy as a result of choosing your company.

- **Call to Action:** It probably seems obvious the next step for your visitor would be to pick up the phone and talk with you. However, if you actually want them to do it, you literally have to spell it out, step by step. With a thousand different distractions, you need to make it simple, clear and direct – call now!

Keep these three elements above the fold.

What's "above the fold?" If you think of a newspaper stand, you'll get the idea. How much of the paper can you see, without picking it up? Whatever it is, it better be spectacular enough to sell copies.

It's the same with your website, but instead of a "fold," there's a scroll down function. Whatever you can see, without scrolling down, is considered above the fold – and it better be attention-grabbing and compelling enough to get your visitors to take action.

What else goes on your landing page?

These two elements should be present in every part of your landing page: a sense of urgency, and a connection to your prospect's pain.

- **Urgency:** You don't want them clicking your ad, landing on your page, and then putting it off for a week. They'll never come back. Instead, give them a reason to call you now, without delay. Maybe you highlight a hidden cost or extra benefit to nudge them to take action now. Maybe offer them a time sensitive discount or bonus.

- **Problem and Pain:** You know how, in real life, the polite thing to do in conversation is to avoid uncomfortable topics? If you stumble onto a sore spot for someone, you do your best to smooth it over and switch to an easier conversation.

In marketing, in a sense, you want to do the opposite. You want to seek out, probe, and push on the pain points a bit to get your prospect to take action. It's for their own good, of course – by turning to your company to fix their problem, it's a win for everyone: for them because they get a solution that works; for you because you just got a new and loyal customer or driver. Your landing page needs to nail the pain points with a direct hit. Again, it's about your message to market match – the people who visit your landing pages don't want to just feel better, and they don't want to know how to fix their problems… they just want them fixed. Now. Make sure your text aligns with what you know they want – an assurance their pain will go away with a call to you.

- **Social Proof:** A crowd attracts a crowd. People like doing business with businesses people like. Those are the ideas behind social proof, and you desperately need this in marketing your products, services, and opportunities.

Here's the best way I know to explain it. We'll use an example you might not know a lot about – and that's perfect.

Pretend you've been sent out to buy a baby stroller for your daughter's baby shower. It's sort of an emergency, because somehow this got overlooked, your wife's too busy with last minute party details, and she's counting on you to come through for her. You manage to find a store that sells them, and are instantly overwhelmed because you're facing a whole aisle filled with strollers in all different sizes, colors, price points, and seemingly different features. The sales clerk sees a sitting duck and starts recommending the model that costs a thousand dollars, stressing how important all the various features are.

You begin to panic.

One particular stroller catches your attention and you start checking it out, hoping the sales clerk will leave you alone. Out of the corner of your eye, you see a lady approaching you. She remarks that she's GOT that stroller you're looking at, loves it, gave the same one to her sister when she had a baby, and that all her kids, who of course rode in that stroller, are lovely, well-behaved darlings… all because of that stroller. (Well, okay, you get the idea.) You buy it immediately.

Hearing from a real, live happy customer carries a lot more weight than anything a salesperson can say. Other customers have no stake in whether you buy. They don't get a commission. They have no reason not to be honest.

That's social proof. It's regular people talking you up for no other reason than that they really like how you helped them.

There are a number of ways you can build social proof into your landing pages. Some of them are harder to do than others, but they're all valuable in building your credibility and putting your prospective customers at ease so they'll feel comfortable calling you.

- **Testimonials.** That's the social proof gold mine. This could be real drivers' real words about signing on with you, and how driving for you has improved their family's life. You can't make this stuff up (literally… you'll get in a lot of trouble if you do). You can't imagine how powerful it is for a prospect to read or watch (yes, video testimonials!) some other regular guy's story about how you saved the day. They know they can trust a regular guy more than some salesperson or actor – and they'll follow that example and call you.

  It can be tricky getting testimonials, though. You need to get them the right way so you don't land in hot water with the FTC. You've got to have certain pieces of information in them to make them believable and not seem like paid advertisements. Make sure you know what you're doing before you publish testimonials, because they'll do wonders for your bottom line if you do it right – but cause you a lot of headaches if you do it wrong.

- **Industry Logos.** People are very visual creatures. Informal studies show that even small children are able to identify an astonishing number of corporate logos. Logos convey a sense of authority and credibility. They communicate that a larger organization has approved a smaller one.

  For example, you may have permission to feature the logos of the carriers you serve. You'll need to check before using them, but that's a powerful endorsement if you can include them on your landing pages.

- **Trust Logos.** It's the same idea with these other logos, but they give credibility about your business practices rather than your products and skills.

  If you've got a stellar Better Business Bureau rating, you should feature the BBB's easily recognizable logo on your landing pages. That communicates to your prospects that you are trustworthy and that other people have used your products and services and gotten good results. While most consumer advice out there on the Internet recommends that people check the BBB before hiring a business, only a small segment of consumers will actually do it – and if they see that BBB logo on your landing page, they'll assume you've got a positive rating.

Another trust logo you should include on your landing pages is a graphic of the credit cards you accept – if that's relevant for you. This is important because not only does it communicate that payment will be easy – even if they don't have cash on hand – it also gives a buyer confidence that yours is a reputable business. Merchant accounts aren't just a matter of signing up; a business has to be vetted before it can accept payments by credit card. Also, should there be an issue, credit and debit card users know they can request help from the card issuer in getting resolution.

All of these trust logos add to the perceived credibility of your business, and help your prospective customers feel more comfortable calling you and working with you. It's about legitimately borrowing the credibility of a larger, more widely known and trusted organization.

- **Your Irresistible Offer:** One of the surest ways to succeed in business is to offer what people really, really want in a way that they know they'd be crazy not to accept your offer. An irresistible offer is so good that they know they won't find a better offer no matter how hard they look, and that they'd just be wasting their own time if they tried to beat it. It's also got to have a level of reasonableness, though – you don't want to cross the line over into making an offer that's "too good to be true" because that'll work against you.

Conventional wisdom about landing pages – at least in other fields – is to use a headline that sparks curiosity and gets people to keep reading. It's not like that in the trucking industry. In our case, you want your irresistible offer right, smack, at the top of your landing page. You want it to give enough information at a glance that someone who's searching can make a fast decision to take action without a second thought.

What goes into making an irresistible offer?

Think about the top considerations people have when they call. Just a few examples:

- **Price** – What's this going to cost me?

    You should consider offering a discount as part of your irresistible offer. Even $25 off is usually enough to ensure you get the call rather than your prospect continuing a search for a better deal.

- **Timing** – How long am I going to have to wait to get this problem fixed?

  Your offer should mention the time issue. Even better if you can back that up by including a location that shows you're right where they are. Many lead gen sites out there are based far, far away and it could be a long wait for a customer before they get a call back ... and even then, it's possible the company doesn't serve the area where that prospect is located. You might also want to mention that a real, live human being will answer their call; that alone is a perk most people only wish for these days.

- **Ability** – Can these guys actually fix the problem, or am I wasting my time?

  Jumping through hoops is bad enough, but what if the prospect goes through a bunch of rigamarole only to find out you can't help them? The goal is to make solving their problem as easy as possible.

- **Design and Usability:** You don't want people who click your ad and go to your landing page to make "THAT" face – you know, the face that looks like someone just tried to make them eat creamed spinach out of a shoe. There are websites out there like that – some of them probably built in the mid 1990's and never updated. They've got neon, blinking and spinning fonts, hideous color schemes, dated photos, and cheesy music that can't be turned off.

That's the extreme, but it goes to illustrate the point that how your landing page looks matters. Make it add to your credibility and encourage your prospects to keep moving forward through your sales funnel, toward calling you. Make your landing page attractive, not repulsive.

Here are some tips:

- Graphics and Photos – Pay for good graphics and photos rather than trying to get by on something you snapped with your phone. Worse yet, don't use free graphics and photos you find online. You may get a nasty letter from whoever took the picture or designed the graphic – or their attorney – telling you that you can't use it without paying for the privilege. You want graphics that go with the color scheme of your logo. You want photos that are modern, attractive, and communicate your "I solve your problems" message.

- Layout – The layout of your landing page is important, too. You want a page that is easy to read, that makes a visitor notice the most important parts first – your irresistible offer, for example. You don't want them to have to wade through paragraphs of text to figure out whether you can help them. Simple is fine – just communicate the information prospects need in order to recognize you can help, and then what they need to know to get in touch with you. You also want to avoid having any navigation on your landing pages. You don't want to give your prospective buyers any other choice but to call. Links to other pages only distract them from what they need to do, which is call you.

- **Structure** – The landing page text should follow this plan:

Above the fold:

- Headline at the top, including your irresistible offer.

- Bullet points with the benefits they get by doing business with you.

- Call to action, giving the simple next step they need to take to hire you.

Under that:

- Testimonials if you've got them.

- Carrier logos

- Trust logos

- Restate your irresistible offer.

One more note about the content of your landing pages.

Think about each funnel set (your ad and your landing page) as a whole. Everything you do should be consistent so the flow from PPC ad to landing page is smooth. You don't want to use different keywords in your ad and on your landing page – they should be the same. You want your ad-clicking prospect to have a seamless experience, not one where they feel like clicking back to the page where they saw your ad to see if maybe they clicked the wrong thing, based on what they found on your landing page.

Oh, and this is a biggie.

Your landing pages need to be mobile friendly. In all likelihood, your prospect is using a smartphone rather than a home computer. Statistics show that mobile usage rates are climbing steadily, already more than 50% of people start their search on a mobile phone. We are always on the go, usually running late, and normally trying to do more than one task at once.

A mobile landing page is easy to navigate with nothing but thumbs. There's no need to pinch and zoom to read the text. There's not a whole lot of text to read. Everything that's truly needed – what would normally be above the fold – is easily visible without thumb-scrolling down or over.

Most important of all, calling your company from a mobile-friendly landing page should be as easy as tapping the screen to start the call.

However, by default, websites and landing pages are not mobile friendly. Maybe your website right now is not mobile friendly. It needs to be specially set up to be optimized and mobile friendly.

The End Result

What's the big payoff from doing all this work? (Because yes, it takes time to create dozens and dozens of highly effective landing pages.)

At least 50%, or 1 out of every 2 people, who come to your landing page should turn into a phone call for you. Now, compared to how most people do it by sending people straight to their Home page, they may only have a 3 to 5% conversion rate, so just 1 out of every 20 people who come to their website end up calling.

All these landing page specs work together to grease your sales funnel and convert searchers into hot leads. There are a lot of details to manage – and it can be especially overwhelming when you realize you're not just making one landing page and calling it a day. You'll need one for every keyword you use in your advertising campaign. It's a big job, and can quickly get unmanageable – but keep reading because you'll see how you may be able to hand off that task later on.

For now, though, the next topic we need to look at is the Pay Per Click ads themselves. If you're going to run ads, you will need to learn how to create ads on AdWords that generate maximum legitimate clicks at minimal cost.

CHAPTER 5

HIT THE HIGHWAY WITH PPC

Here's where we get into the juicy goodness of Pay Per Click advertising through Facebook and through Google's AdWords program.

What's weird is that in SEO, there's a huge focus in the industry on staying ahead of Google, a perception (and it might be accurate) that Google's constantly trying to block traffic from getting to your site, aiming to push you back down off the top of the heap of websites. Google's waging a constant war against getting gamed by people who want to extract free traffic from the search engine giant. It's about the same with Facebook these days, too.

It's a different scene when it comes to paying Google and Facebook to send you traffic.

Look at it this way, where do these companies make money? It's not when you click on the "organic" listings or look at the cute cat pictures your daughter posted, it's when you click on an ad.

All of a sudden, when you're paying for traffic, Google and Facebook become a lot friendlier to work with. After all, they make money every time someone clicks your ads – so they want to be sure your ads have every chance of succeeding. You are now on the same team with Google and Facebook, versus competing against them with SEO.

That's the pond where we're going to fish. That's where you'll get results, which is what matters.

The basic concept is this:

- Figure out how people go searching for what you offer – this is your keyword research.

- Write ads using those keywords and publish online to reach the people most likely to do business with you.

- Make sure those ads show up during the most fruitful time periods.

- Connect those ads to the high-converting landing pages we just talked about.

- Know what to do when the phone starts ringing.

- Serve with excellence.

- Rinse and repeat.

So, some discussion of keywords and keyword research is in order. You might want to grab a cup of coffee – I'll make it as painless as possible, and at least you don't have to DO keyword research right now, but it's not a walk in the park.

Keywords are whatever someone puts into Google to go looking for products, services, and information. Sometimes a keyword is a single word. Sometimes it's actually a string of words or even a question. Keywords that are long are called long-tail keywords, as we mentioned a while ago.

Some weird facts about keywords and how people search for what they need:

- They sometimes use Google like they're asking a Magic 8 Ball toy for advice.

- They often misspell what they're looking for.

- Very few people ever use the "I'm Feeling Lucky" button on Google – wonder why?

- People use different types of keywords when they're shopping around versus when they're about to commit.

Shopping vs. Buying Keywords

Let's talk about that last one for a moment. When prospects are in different phases of the searching and buying cycle, they have different needs and wants.

For example, if you were thinking about starting to see a chiropractor on a regular basis, you might search on Google for information like:

- Benefits of chiropractic

- Do chiropractic adjustments hurt?

- Back exercises to do at home

- Is a chiropractor covered by health insurance?

Kind of all over the place with those searches, because you're just in the information-gathering phase – that's a researcher, someone who's at the top of the sales funnel. There's no particular urgency. You're just as likely to stumble onto free how-to advice you can follow at home to strengthen your back and core as you are to end up in a chiropractor's office.

Once you have this basic information processed, if you decide that seeing a chiropractor still might be a good idea for you, you'd probably start to have some more concrete ideas about how you want to proceed. Your searches would become more specific, one step closer to plunking down cold, hard cash. You're now a shopper.

If you actually threw your back out, you'd move from being a shopper to being a buyer. You'd search for a chiropractor in your city or town, and call the first one that seemed to be taking new patients. If you called an office and a real person answered, was courteous, said you could come in that day, and maybe even offered you a special offer on your first visit, you'd be there with your wallet open as fast as you could get there.

Urgency changes the pace of a prospect going through a sales funnel, makes for far more specific Google searches, and yields the easiest sales for **businesses that can solve problems quickly.**

Broad vs. Specific Keywords

We've talked a bit about the kinds of keywords SEO firms will go after for you and why. They go for broad keywords, like "trucking in Oklahoma City" because they know that even though that's a very competitive keyword (meaning, every SEO guy with a trucking company client in Oklahoma City is going after that keyword), it beats the alternative for them. The alternative would be going after far more specific keywords, such as "Mack fuel gauge repair, Oklahoma City" and that would mean constructing and ranking website pages for every possible combination of manufacturer, carrier, part, and location. For each website page an SEO firm wants to rank, there's an enormous amount of work involved – and clients get tired of paying for all that work with no revenue results.

The great news is that that's not even an issue with PPC advertising. You can and should go very specific with the keywords you use in your campaign.

In fact, the more specific the keyword, the more likely a searcher is to become a buyer or lead very soon, assuming they find the information they need to be able to make the next move.

Tip: Aim for specific keywords rather than general ones in your ads.

Negative Keywords

They're not as bad as they sound, and in this case, it's a great time-saver and money-saver to know about negative keywords.

Negative keywords are words you specifically list that you do not want to trigger your PPC ads. Some great examples include free, cheap, how to, and DIY. For obvious reasons, you don't want your ads showing up for someone who wants free or cheap stuff, or to learn how to fix their problem on their own, or for a product, service, or employment opportunity that's irrelevant to you.

With Google AdWords and Facebook Ads, you can specify a list of words like this. This enables you to make sure your ads don't even show up in front of non-ideal customer prospects.

If there are specifics you get asked about a lot but your business does not offer solutions for, you could add those to your negative keywords list as well.

Tip: Use the negative keyword option to prevent your ad from showing up for non-ideal prospects.

Don't Build One Big, Dumb Campaign

With PPC advertising, there's a term that's important – your campaign. Within your overall advertising plan for PPC, you can build campaigns – it's a way of structuring your strategy.

Most advertisers – at least the ones who have a hard time getting good results – build what I'll call a big, dumb campaign. In trucking marketing, this would look like lumping all the carriers they service, all their service locations, all the manufacturers and brands all into one big pile.

It's the equivalent of packing a trunk full of every object you might need throughout the day – including your tools, your meals, your clothing, truck keys, that sticky note from your kid asking if you can have pizza for dinner… everything. Then, every time you need one thing from your trunk, you have to sort through and hunt for it. Add to it the complication that sometimes you'll need to look at every item in there to make sure everything's working as planned – and to be able to remove or modify something if it's not performing.

Instead, pack it all into an organized, expandable, compartmentalized box. This will allow you to find what you need in seconds, make modifications to it on a micro level, evaluate precisely what's working and what's not, and to add on without fear of duplication or confusion. You want an ultra-targeted advertising campaign.

Yes, it's a lot more to manage this way. It's a far more sophisticated system than just chucking stuff into one big box. But its precision makes for dramatically better results.

Structuring Your Campaign

So, how do you structure a smart PPC campaign?

1. Start with keyword research. Gather every possible keyword combination you can find.

2. Put your keywords into groups. Start with the more basic keywords, then make groups by location, each carrier, each brand, and then each product or service combination.

3. Put the keywords together in every variation of word order possible. For example, truck fuel discounts in Oklahoma City is significantly different in Google's eyes from Oklahoma City truck fuel discounts.

4. Next, you build what AdWords refers to as campaigns. They are built around your keyword groups.

5. Write ads for each keyword combination.

6. Link your ads to your landing pages. Each keyword combination should have a corresponding landing page, as we've discussed.

About Writing Your Ads

You need to create a highly-targeted ad with a strong call to action – but you have very limited space to write the ad. Your headline can only have 25 characters, including spaces. You get two description lines, each with a maximum of 35 characters, including spaces. Then, the display URL (the website address you want to show in your ad) is also limited to 35 characters that will be visible – you can enter a longer URL, but it will be shortened.

There are a LOT of rules for how your ad has to be written – and if it's not to Google's liking, it will be rejected.

Your ad doesn't have a lot of space to work with. You need to make every character count. Every word must move your prospects closer to buying.

Include your call to action in your ad. Include your phone number (remember, you've got to have a phone number you use only for these ads so you can track their effectiveness). Include some sort of "limiting language" (for example, "Call Before 3 p.m. to Get $500 Signing Bonus") in the ad to create a sense of urgency. This will help ensure the prospect calls you today rather than waiting until next week.

Ramp It Up with Extensions

Ad extensions are a new feature that adds dimension and depth to your ad. There are a few types of extensions you need to understand:

- Call extensions: These let you display your phone number right in your ad, giving your prospect a direct path to call you.

- Site link extensions: These allow you to include up to four links to other pages of your website. You can also highlight special offers or calls to action using site link extensions.

- Ad extensions: These increase the size of your ad, which draws extra attention to it and separates you from your competition.

All of these extensions are great ways to increase your leads and lower your costs.

Your Quality Score

There's a test. Not just the test of going live with your PPC ads and seeing how much revenue they bring in – there's an actual department at Google that's evaluating your ads. They look at how well your ad text matches up to your keyword, and how well that all matches up to a Google searcher's search. They also look at your landing pages, how quickly they load, how long someone stays on your landing page, what keywords are on there, and probably some other factors nobody knows about in detail.

If you get a positive Quality Score, you will get better conversion rates, lower advertising rates, and your ads will show up in better spots more often.

There are many ways to improve your Quality Score, but here are the first steps you'll need to take to get it as high as you can:

1. Know what your Quality Scores are. You can find that information by logging into your AdWords account, selecting a campaign, looking at the Keywords tab, click on Columns on that toolbar, then clicking Customize Columns. Then you should be able to see the Quality Score. Phew.

2. Organize your keywords really well. You want to keep your AdGroups small – maybe only a handful of different keywords in each. Make sure they all relate closely to each other.

3. Make sure your ads and landing pages match the keywords in each AdGroup. This means those keywords should appear in the ad and the landing page as well as in your AdGroup. Remember not to use your Home page – that will NOT yield good results for you. The ads have to

lead to specific landing pages that are focused on the particular keywords you use in the ad.

When you start doing PPC advertising for your trucking company, you enter a never-ending quest for achieving better Quality Scores. It'll be official – you'll turn into a total geek, and nobody will want to talk to you at parties anymore.

But you'll start getting more leads calling than ever before, so it might be worth it.

In the next chapter, we'll talk about a more human element in this advertising strategy – what to do when the phone starts ringing.

CHAPTER 6

ON THE HORN WITH PPC

The moment of truth – your phone begins ringing. A lot.

We've talked some about the whole process of getting new customers and leads as being your sales funnel. At the top, you've got people who are somehow involved in the trucking industry, but who aren't looking for what you offer right now.

In the middle of the funnel, these folks are starting to realize they've got a problem. Maybe their current job isn't working out. Maybe their drivers are facing a particular challenge you solve. What they're doing now is technically still working... but they're starting to become more aware of their impending need to fix the situation. They might start looking for a solution, but might not get around to making a phone call. Not every lead goes through this phase, of course – sometimes there's no warning before it all goes haywire.

That point where something's broken is the bottom of the funnel. It's action time. The question at that point is not whether something's wrong, it's who to call to get it fixed. That's when they're most likely to encounter your PPC ad and call you.

At that moment, when they dial your number, they exit the sales funnel and fall into a bucket, where they'll be yours for as long as you can keep them happy – unless they fall out of the bucket.

What determines whether you get to keep these "almosts" is what happens when they call you.

Do this part right, and you're likely to have a long-term customer who sends other leads your way. Do it wrong, and you'll waste all the money and effort that went into creating and running your PPC advertisement – because you'll be left standing there watching your "almost customer" or "almost driver" go to your competitor instead.

Your phone process is that important.

I've trained a lot of my clients' offices on how to turn almost every phone call that comes in into a success, and I'll share the highlights with you in just a moment.

First, there's something you need to put into place before you get even one phone call from your advertising.

Call Tracking

Remember back in the old days of advertising in the newspaper or Yellow Pages? As a sophisticated advertiser, you knew you needed to have a designated phone number that appeared just in your ad. This would allow you to measure how effective that advertising investment was – you'd know exactly how many phone calls came in as a result of placing your ad.

It's the same with your PPC advertising.

If you're not tracking your calls, it's impossible to know for sure what's working and what's not. How else will you know where your calls came from, or which ads generated the most calls?

You certainly can't count on the person answering your phone to get that information! They may not remember to ask, and even if they do, there's absolutely no way that the caller will remember

– accurately – where they saw your ad, what they typed into Google, when they saw it, which landing page they went to…

You see what I mean?

So, you'll need to come up with a way to track your calls. Best practice would be to have a different phone number associated with each ad you're running – but we've already talked about how many ads you're going to need to run… one for every combination of appliance, brand, and location.

That's a lot of phone numbers.

It can be done, and it's really important to do. But, doing it manually like that is a task that's so big it could easily take several employees to manage.

What some companies do is use some unique software to provide custom call tracking in our dashboard. With this software, you can see exactly which ad, which keyword, which landing page produced the call – at a glance. You can tell how many calls you get, how much you're paying for the ad that produced those calls, and what changes to make to get even better results.

OK, so for sure you're going to want to find a call tracking solution like that.

Now, onto the phone answering system...

The Simple Phone Script System

It's like gathering fruit, this whole process of getting new leads to fall into your basket. I noticed that with some of my clients, no matter how much website traffic they got, no matter how many phone calls they got, they still seemed to drop a lot of fruit on the ground.

Some receptionists were great at converting these calls into wins – their close rate was phenomenal. Others, even though they were friendly and professional, seemed to end way too many calls without getting the desired result. Still others had very inconsistent results – sometimes they'd succeed, and other times the caller would hang up after saying they'd shop around a bit more and maybe call back.

Everyone who owns a business knows that the person answering your phones is doing one of the most important jobs in your business. They are the first human contact a customer has with your business. They are the one closing – or not.

Of course, you want the person answering your phones to be polite, friendly, professional, and for callers to get such a good impression of your business from that one phone call that they want to do business with you.

That's not enough, though.

I've studied proven sales processes, scripts, and psychology enough to have learned some really important lessons that can change your results dramatically. See, just like your marketing works like a funnel, the phone call is the same – the goal is to make your lead's process of going from dialing to doing business smooth. You want to eliminate bumps and holes in the funnel that would result in the call ending without the results you want.

That's why I created what I call the Simple Phone Script System. It's built on 7 simple rules for every phone call and 5 magic questions. It simplifies the process of turning leads into wins. It also sets up a standard system to follow so that you get results you can count on. Using a system like this, you know that if you generate X number of phone calls, you'll land Y results. It's all about getting consistent results.

It makes the process more scientific, and by following the proven process you can replicate your results over and over.

Leads Are Meaningless On Their Own

Why does this matter so much? Remember – you can generate leads all day long, but if you can't convert them into results, there's no point. It's a complete waste of time and money to run marketing campaigns if you can't close.

You've got to close the gap between a lead and actual money. Leads are ultimately meaningless. You can't buy groceries with leads. You can't pay with leads to take a vacation with your family. No doctor on the planet accepts leads as a form of payment when you've got a sick child.

You get the idea. You've got to turn that lead into money-making results.

We'll get into HOW to do that in just a minute. But first we probably should talk a little about WHY.

My Simple Phone Script System, like I said, is designed to work WITH human psychology to produce a certain result: The caller takes the action you want them to take.

The process works by triggering certain responses in your caller that help build a feeling of knowing, liking, and trusting your trucking company. At every step throughout the process, the caller is gently nudged toward taking action.

Some people might wonder if there's an ethical problem with that, if it's manipulative or otherwise shady.

Here's the thing:

- Your prospective customer has a real problem.

- They need someone to help them – for real.

- They need that help now.

- They need to be able to trust that it's all going to turn out right.

- They need to feel comfortable with the next action they take.

- They need to know they're not being ripped off.

So, as a trucking company with high integrity, a commitment to providing excellence, and the certainty that you offer the best possible option for this lead, how do you best serve this person?

By doing all you can to make doing business with you easy and comfortable?

Or…

Leaving it up to chance that the lead will be served well (by you), or potentially ripped off (by someone else)?

It might sound a little crazy to be this passionate about a phone script, or even about trucking services – but not if you remember what it is you're actually selling. You sell problem solving, the restoration of a family's peace of mind.

The best way to serve your customers is to make it easy for them to let you serve them!

That said, here's the basic gist of the Simple Phone Script System.

Every time a prospective customer calls your business, you want to accomplish the following:

Get them talking about their situation right away. This situation is causing problems. It's a pain for them. It's frustrating and aggravating and wrecking their entire daily routine.

It's been said that, "People love to buy stuff... they just don't like being sold." And it's true – no matter how motivated you are to buy something, when a salesperson is pushing you to buy, you're turned off.

It's far more effective when folks sell themselves on the solution you offer. Buying decisions are emotional – especially when they involve stopping something that's causing pain. The decision to buy comes from emotion; then the brain works to justify that decision.

So, if you can get the caller to spill their guts about what's going on, they'll start the process of selling themselves on your solutions.

Encourage them to vent. It's not enough to say, "My drivers are spending way too much money on fuel." You want them to go into more detail about when they first noticed the problem, what other problems this is causing. The more they talk about how bad this problem is, the more they sell themselves on getting it fixed. This also positions you as someone they begin to know, like, and trust – you're more of a confidant than a salesperson. You're with them in their time of need.

Get a little personal. At the right time, you'll want to start getting more personal information – starting with their name, and a bit later, their address. Getting this information accomplishes two important goals in the call.

First, by using someone's name, you strengthen the connection with them. If you think about it, people behave oddly when they're anonymous, but not when they've given their name. You're more likely to get tire kickers when the caller remains anonymous because there's no sense of accountability.

Second, by asking for your caller's name, you set a pattern for the conversation. The pattern is that you are leading the conversation, and that when you make offers or requests, they'll say yes. You ask for their name, they give it. Ultimately, you offer an appointment, and they take it.

Offer choices that all lead to a win. Along the lines of leading the conversation, when you offer the next step – say, an appointment with your salesperson or driver recruiter, you want to offer it in a way that is easy for them to say yes. So, offer it in a way that "no" becomes a strange reply. For example, "Would morning or afternoon work better for you?" is more likely to result in an appointment than a "no". Remember, the goal is to serve your customer with excellence – and you can't do that if they won't take the next step.

Get the appointment scheduled – that's the whole goal. You're not trying to sell anything in this first contact. You're only selling the appointment. The appointment is the next step, and only after you've gone out for the appointment can you sell whatever comes next.

It would be a really good idea to take a close look at the phone script your receptionist is following, and to evaluate it based on this advice. Take a look at the closing rate you're getting with that script – How many calls come in? How many end up with the result you want? Is there room for improvement?

If so, now you'll probably be thinking about how the Simple Phone Script System could turn things around for you. In fact, you might even be wondering how you could get your hands on it. If you promise to stay focused long enough to finish reading, I'll make you a promise – you'll find out how you can get the whole Simple Phone Script System absolutely free. Deal?

In the Simple Phone Script System, you'll get:

- The complete phone script I've developed for trucking companies that is proven to result in better results.

- The 5 magic questions you need to ask, word for word, on each phone call that comes in.

- The 7 rules you must follow for every phone call to dramatically improve your results.

The beauty of having a system like this is that it's foolproof. In the hands of a great receptionist, this system will help you accomplish what every trucking company out there only wishes they could have:

A surefire way to turn leads into wins.

All that you've read up until now sets the foundation for you to create a marketing system so powerful that you can easily bring in new business or drivers every day – like pulling a lever as many times as you want to increase your revenues at will. Next up, though, you'll learn one thing you can do – that probably NONE of your competitors is doing – that can yield exponentially bigger numbers for you.

CHAPTER 7

YOUR ADS REQUIRE REGULAR TUNE-UPS

Great news! At this point in your reading, you've learned enough about building a Pay Per Click advertising system for your trucking company that you can see the potential for easily doubling or tripling your profits in the coming year.

Even better news… you've reached the chapter that will explain how you can take the amazing results your PPC advertising can produce and make them even better.

This is all about optimization, which is the process of making tiny little changes that lead to exponentially better results.

This is also the part where you'll either geek out over the brilliance of the process – or else your eyes will glaze over and you'll realize that this is a task you never want to try on your own.

Either way, you need to know just enough to make yourself dangerous. Whether you take this on in-house or hire someone to do it for you, you need to at least understand the basics.

Optimization is a scientific, methodical process of discovering what's working best in your PPC sales funnel so you can do more of what's working and less of what's not working.

Perry Marshall, the famous marketer, said, "Everybody knows half your advertising budget is being wasted… it's just a matter of determining which half."

The optimizing process involves split testing EVERYTHING: ads, landing pages, offers to see what's working best. It involves making a single, small change to one of these elements to see whether the original or the new version performs best. Once you have a winner, you try to beat it with a new,

new version. This process goes on indefinitely, with the constant goal of getting better results.

In traditional advertising, optimization would work by running multiple Yellow Pages ads using a different phone number for each ad. If you've ever tried to do something like that, you know it's super-expensive and can quickly get crazy as you try to keep track of what number went with which ad.

How on earth are you supposed to know whether your ad will work? By the time you figure out how it's working, it's too late – and forget about comparing multiple ads. You can't run ads side by side, either; to get feedback on two different ads, you'd need to be in two similar publications. In the end, you'd eventually figure out whether your ad worked, but it would be too late to course-correct, and you can easily end up stuck with an under-performing ad running for months and months.

With digital marketing, we've got a unique opportunity. You aren't stuck with some little 2" x 2" ad, locked in for a whole year before you can even change it. Instead, with PPC advertising, you can test as you go. Your landing pages, colors, layout, ad copy, offer... every element of your advertising matters.

Digital marketing is far more maneuverable than traditional print marketing. You can literally run a test on two versions of your ad, determine that one version is outperforming the other, and then shift your budget to the one that's working better – all on the spot. You can zero in on what's working, making small improvements to each element so you get better performance and an increasing ROI over time

For my clients, we split test and optimize for the following variables in their PPC funnel:

- Ad budget
- Locations
- Time of day
- Day of the week
- Keywords
- Negative keywords
- Ad position
- Split-test ads
- Split-test landing pages
- We even optimize for mobile phones and tablets

Essentially, we break the new customer getting process down to a granular level. At every point along the way, every time there's an encounter with a prospect, we perform a split test. We alter one small element and observe the results. Because you can get real time numbers, you can quickly determine what's working and what's not. This allows you to improve the effectiveness of each ad, landing page, and offer – and when you multiply small, incremental improvements, you end up with big gains overall.

Of course, that's if you do it right.

Again, I don't want to drag you too far into the mad scientist world of optimization, but just want you to understand enough to realize the potential that's available for a marketer who's got a powerful grasp of these intricate little parts and processes. It took me years of study to learn all this – and since it's my thing, I actually enjoy running these split tests and seeing what's actually performing well. (Weird, I know.)

It helps that I've got a whole team at my disposal: graphic designers, landing page builders, Facebook and AdWords advisors, copywriting experts. All these different skills and specialties are needed to make split testing and optimization work. It's an insane amount of work, but it's worth it when

I see my clients' ads produce better and better results for them.

Probably NOT a Good DIY Project

I have known business owners who decided this seemed like a good project for them to take on. They figured they could do it in-house and that even though it would be time-consuming, it would yield results that would make the effort pay off. Unfortunately, they quickly discovered that while getting better and better results is the goal, sometimes when a split test isn't run correctly, they can end up with worse results. Sometimes they broke stuff in their funnel along the way. Sometimes they made multiple changes at a time, and then couldn't tell with any certainty at all which changes caused the much better – or much worse – results.

Running split tests requires you to be meticulous, scientific, and very patient. Only with a true A/B split test process can you determine valid gains and losses.

You've also got to know what to split test, and in what order. If you're testing variables that are irrelevant, you'll waste a lot of time. If you test in the wrong order, you'll set yourself up for failure because each step along the way builds on the results of the prior step.

Successful split testing requires a lot of resources – and probably more than a little obsessiveness. Done right, all the effort pays off big time; done incorrectly, this could be the biggest headache you ever gave yourself.

Many of our clients say that just being able to avoid ever having to run split tests or learning the finer points of optimization was reason enough for them to outsource their PPC advertising to my team. It's not that it's a truly horrible experience – it's just that there's a lot that can go wrong, a lot to learn before you dive in, and that it takes significant skills and experience to get the best possible results.

Whether you want to take this part of the process on by yourself (probably not), or you'd rather just entrust it to someone who knows what they're doing and does it every day, you'll want to get the information that's coming in the next chapter.

CHAPTER 8

HOW TO WORK WITH US

Here's where we break into two camps...

It's possible you've gotten this far and come to the conclusion that you'd like to give this PPC stuff a try on your own. Crazy, but okay; I hope the information I've given you will help you get excellent results from the hard work you're about to put in. It's definitely possible you could learn how to do all this on your own. Not the best use of your time and resources, but some people just really like to do things on their own.

Most likely, though, you're not crazy, and realize that the smartest move would be to outsource this whole thing to someone who knows what they're doing. You've spent years working and learning to run your trucking business. It's not a quick or easy process to accumulate that amount of wisdom, and most likely you learned the most from the times you made mistakes. You probably realize the value of having someone who's already gone through the learning curve of PPC advertising for this business, who's got the experience, team, and real world training to get great results.

You know that you make the most money, and suffer the fewest headaches, when you stick to what you do best – running your trucking business. Any task not directly related to that, you're best off handing off to someone else who specializes in that task.

That's why you'll want to hear about our system. It's like having your very own lead generation machine where you get to keep 100% of the leads in your area rather than fighting over them with your competitors. You even get a dedicated AdWords Manager who never stops working to make sure you get the best leads at the cheapest price.

Here's what makes up our system:

A Shockingly Good Track Record

You pay for results, not to underwrite our education.

After getting outstanding results in the trucking industry, we've learned the market, learned the business, and learned the customer – that means you get all the benefits of that market research from day one.

Full Speed Ahead, Right Away

You don't waste time and money on trial and error.

We know what works. We know what doesn't work. We only do what works… and we only do it for trucking companies. What could be simpler? By working with a trucking industry marketing specialist, you'll see great results faster and with far less risk than you'd have in working with a generalist who's got to learn the ropes before getting a good ROI.

You're 7 Days Away from Results

Forget waiting patiently for the phone to ring.

Any SEO firm with integrity admits it will take 6-9 months to get results. Any trucking company owner knows 6-9 months is way too long to pay for a tactic that's not producing new business. Time is money.

With this System, we guarantee you'll start seeing results within 7 days.

Shared, Warmed-Over Leads? Never Again!

You can kiss those ridiculously priced leads goodbye forever.

Rest stop racks, temp agencies, and job boards – all those shared leads programs charge a fortune and all you're guaranteed is a crack at the leads that come in… along with anyone else who's bought that privilege. With our system, you don't have to share. The leads are yours, 100%. Your competitor wants to home in on your leads? Forget it! When you work with us, you lock that guy out of the action.

Not an ATM, but Pretty Close

Your very own lead generation machine.

As our client, you'll get your own private-label lead generation engine. This goes way beyond having a website, or generating a huge amount of traffic, or even buying a list of leads. This is a non-stop lead generation machine that produces highly-targeted leads, people who are standing there ready to take action – all they need is to find you.

Money, Meet Mouth

How about an "absolutely nothing to lose" guarantee?

There are thousands of marketing agencies out there, hundreds that actually know what they're doing, and maybe a handful that might know a thing or two about the trucking industry. However, here's something completely unique to our system: a guarantee that your results will be spectacular. In fact, you'll see revenue streaming in within your first week – and we guarantee you'll be in the black on this investment within the first 30 days or you get your money back. You won't find guarantees like that anywhere else.

We Count What Counts

Revenue is the true measure of success, not leads.

More premium customers, excellent drivers, better quality leads, and fewer tire kickers – these elements combine to produce higher revenues for your trucking company. Once you start seeing revenue stream in from your partnership with us, you'll wonder why on earth you ever thought paying for leads was a good idea. It's all about revenue.

We Do All the Heavy Lifting

Your dedicated marketing manager works the magic so you can grow.

You don't have to lift a finger to create your PPC campaigns, build your landing pages, craft your offers, or optimize each step in your funnel. All you've got to do is continue providing an excellent experience to every prospect and customer who calls you. Run your trucking business, make money. Leave the rest to us and focus on what you do best.

Our System is Unique – in 3 Ways

1. We ONLY work with trucking companies

We are the ONLY PPC agency that works only with trucking companies. By focusing only on trucking companies, we've gone through the learning curve. We know your business. We know your customers. We know what works, and what doesn't. You pay for results – not to bring us up to speed.

2. A 100% success rate

Our proven marketing system is currently profitable in trucking markets all across the United States – with an astonishing 100% success rate. There are few guarantees in life and business, but we offer one that's rock solid because we are so certain we'll make you a positive ROI… fast.

3. Exclusivity in your area

Forget squabbling over lame leads with your competitor. When you partner with us, you get 100% of the leads that come in in your area. You control the entire market. You lock out your competition – we simply won't work with them.

Here's what you get when you become our exclusive partner in your area:

- A Proven Marketing System from Day One
- 100% Exclusivity in Your Area
- Custom Domain Name
- Custom AdWords Account
- Custom Facebook Account
- Advanced Keyword Research
- New Website & Landing Pages
- Professional Copywriting
- Custom Call Tracking Phone Number

- Dedicated Facebook, AdWords & Business Consultant

- Lead Conversion Coaching/Training

- Ongoing Optimization for Strategic Growth & Max Profits

- Monthly Analytics Reports

Oh, and You Didn't Think We'd Forget the Super Simple Phone System, Did You?

You get it in all its appointment-generating goodness. The phone rings, your bank account fills up. It's yours absolutely free as our client, and we can't wait to hear about how it changes your business when every time the phone rings, your odds of getting an appointment recruit or sale skyrocket.

What to Do Next

If you're struggling with your marketing, you're probably paying too much only to get less than desirable results. You're frustrated and overwhelmed. You're working hard to get results and by all accounts, according to what 'everyone' out there says, you're doing everything you should be… but it's not working.

It's not your fault, though. You've just believed some of the most common myths about trucking industry marketing that are out there. The truth is, it doesn't matter how hard you work at content marketing and SEO. All those will do – if you work hard enough – is to get you top rankings on Google and a lot of website traffic. While those sound good, we all know that what really counts is REVENUE. If you get that, if you've learned enough about this completely unique system to understand how it could completely transform and explode your trucking business, then we should talk.

We only work with a very select group of trucking companies. Because of our commitment to exclusivity, we can only take on one partner per service area, so we'll need to have a quick introductory chat to see whether we should continue talking.

Let's set up a time to talk and see whether this makes sense for your business. You have absolutely nothing to lose.

You can reach me at:

Email: landon@dbsdvantage.com
Phone: 405.973.8002

About the Author

Landon Middleton is a proud husband of over 15 years to his beautiful wife, Jessica. They live in Oklahoma City with their four lovely children, Andrew, Alec, Ames and Amri.

Landon has been in digital marketing and trucking for nearly 10 years, serving on the front lines for his clients in trucking through state associations, national organizations, large corporations, major truck shows and even in front of Congress on Capitol Hill.

Landon has a passion to change the culture of customer acquisition and driver recruiting in the trucking industry by delivering an authentic service to his clients that they own 100%, bringing costs of marketing way down and results way up!

www.ingramcontent.com/pod-product-compliance
Lightning Source LLC
Chambersburg PA
CBHW070314230526
45470CB00002B/868